SEP - 7 2011

Kisstory

Kisstory

A Sweet and Sexy Look
at the History of Kissing

Joanne Wannan

RUNNING PRESS
PHILADELPHIA · LONDON

Library of Congress Control Number: 2009920973

ISBN 978-0-7624-3785-6

Designed by Maria Taffera Lewis, Blue Studio Design
Edited by Jordana Tusman
Typography: Goudy Old Style, Monotype Corsiva and Black Chancery
Cover image: *The Kiss*, detail of painting by G. Baldry. ©Simon Carter Gallery, Woodbridge, Suffolk, UK/The Bridgeman Art Library

Running Press Book Publishers
2300 Chestnut Street
Philadelphia, PA 19103-4371

Visit us on the web!
www.runningpress.com

354
W

❦ Table of Contents ❧

Introduction

THE DECISION TO KISS FOR THE FIRST TIME IS THE MOST CRUCIAL IN ANY LOVE STORY. IT CHANGES THE RELATIONSHIP OF TWO PEOPLE MUCH MORE STRONGLY THAN EVEN THE FINAL SURRENDER; BECAUSE THIS KISS ALREADY HAS WITHIN IT THAT SURRENDER.

—Emil Ludwig

h, kissing. It represents so many things to so many people. It can be a greeting, a token of love and affection, or in the case of Judas and the criminal underworld, a sign of betrayal. There are goodnight kisses, candy kisses, and kisses that can wake up a Sleeping Beauty or turn a toad into a charming prince.

Kisses are the language of love, so let's talk it over. —American proverb

But what do we really know about kissing? How is it that this simple movement of the lips has come to take on such great significance in our lives that a kiss can convey, perhaps far better than words, our innermost feelings, secret desires, and very personal life stories?

There's no record of the world's first kiss, but it may have looked something like this: The sun is setting over Stone Age Land. Two people are seen in the distance approaching each other, smiling, looking deep into each other's eyes. Then they lean forward . . . and lick each other's cheeks! Yes, that's right. According to one theory, the first "kiss" had a very practical purpose: to obtain salt, which was in short supply.

But other researchers scoff at the correlation, pointing out that not all cultures kiss. In fact, some hadn't even heard of it before coming into contact with European civilization. Tribes in sub-Saharan Africa, the Australian aboriginals, and Native Americans didn't kiss. Nor did Finnish tribes, even though members of both sexes would bathe together naked.

Other cultures rub noses. "Eskimo kissing," as it is sometimes called, occurs not only among the Inuit, but in Polynesia, Malaysia, and the South Pacific, as well.

The word "kiss" in Old English is *cyssan*. It comes from the Germanic word *kussjan* or *kuss*, probably because of the sound a kiss makes. Ninety percent of the world's population kisses, and the average person spends 336 hours (that's two whole weeks!) of their lives puckering up. But why do we kiss? Well, there's a branch of science that studies kissing called philematology, and researchers have shaped some fascinating theories.

Lips, it seems, were made for kissing. Lips have the thinnest skin layer of all parts of the body and are a hundred times more sensitive than the fingertips. The tongue and interior of the mouth also contain an abundant nerve supply. Nerves from these areas transfer messages directly to the limbic system, which is the oldest part of the brain and is associated with sexual pleasure.

Another theory is that when we kiss, we transfer sebum, a substance that lubricates our skin and hair. Sebum is chemically addictive, so while this sentiment isn't likely to find its way into Valentine's cards or songs anytime soon ("Hey baby, I love your sebum!" or "I'm saving all my sebum for you!"), it may be the reason that a good kiss will keep us coming back for more.

Researchers have found that a man's saliva contains the male

❦ The Birds Do It ❦

Expressions of affection are actually quite common in the animal world. Snails rub their antennae before mating, even though they mate only once in their lives. Dolphins and moles sniff each other, as does your family dog. Even chimpanzees give each other platonic pecks on the cheeks.

Other animals aren't quite as discreet. Canadian porcupines kiss each other on the mouth. (Extra caution is needed to avoid the quills!) The Kissing Gourami, a large tropical fish with protruding lips, not only kisses other Gourami, but plants and other objects as well. And two red pandas at a Tokyo zoo created "panda-monium" with their displays of affection. They would engage in mouth-to-mouth kissing on a regular basis, as astonished visitors looked on. Marathon

hormone testosterone, putting his partner in the mood for love. And studies show that females unconsciously assess a man's health via his saliva and breath. For both partners, a satisfying smooch releases adrenaline, as well as oxytocin. Oxytocin is a hormone that causes our breath to get shallow and our heart to skip a beat. It's the same hormone that is released during strenuous exercise, when doing high-risk activities like parachuting and bungee jumping.

At any rate, one thing we *do* know for sure—we kiss because it feels *so* good!

make-out sessions lasted up to an hour at a time!

Bonobo apes, our closest genetic cousins, take it one step further. They exchange sloppy open-mouthed French kisses regardless of sex, age, or status. They kiss to relieve stress and to form bonds. And sometimes they just kiss for no apparent reason at all!

that the breath contained the spirit, the very essence of life. A kiss was considered so powerful that it was often associated with giving life. In the Old Testament, God "kissed" man, infusing him with life.

The truth is, there's not a lot of reference to romantic kissing in ancient times. That doesn't mean that people didn't do it, just that artists and writers might have considered it too private (or too risqué) to record.

Nose kissing was the highest form of affection in Egypt. The word for kiss translates as "scent."

Even Cleopatra, with her many lovers, is believed never to have kissed on the lips.

In ancient times, there were also kisses of greeting and of respect. Egyptians would kiss the ground the Pharaohs walked on; or if they were lucky, maybe even his toe! And as for the first "air kisses," Pagans worshipped their gods by blowing kisses to them.

The ancients really had it covered when it came to kissing . . . or so it seems. But what about a good old lip-lock of the delicious, sensuous kind? Well, hang onto

❦ French Kissing ❧

Deep kissing has been around for a long time. It is mentioned in the *Kama Sutra*, which called it the "fighting of the tongue." In the ancient Chinese Tao tradition, a perfect balance of yin and yang is achieved by the exchange of "liquid jade" (or, less poetically—saliva!).

The term "French kiss" was first used in the English language around 1923. It was actually a slur on the French, who were regarded as overly amorous. The French, however, don't use that term. Instead, they refer to it as "tongue kissing," "soul kissing," or in slang, *rouler une pelle* ("to roll a shovel") or *rouler un patin* ("to skate").

In Britain and Ireland, deep kissing is called "snogging." Italians use the term *limonare* ("to lemon"). In Quebec, it is known as *frencher*. In Spain, the term is *morrear* ("to muzzle") or *rumbear* ("to party"). And if you hook up in Western cultures, you might find yourself playing tongue hockey or swapping spit!

In Southern India, the "French kiss" is known as the "English kiss." Since Indian films didn't show deep kissing, the only time Indians saw it was in British films.

your breath mints! We're headed for that!

The earliest written record of mouth kissing comes from India. There, Vedic Sanskrit texts dating back to 150 BC describe kissing, as does the *Vatsyayana Kamasutrum* or *Kama Sutra*, which was originally passed down orally (no pun intended) before it was later recorded in Sanskrit. It is an ancient book of knowledge dedicated to Kama, the Hindu god of love.

The *Kama Sutra* (or "aphorisms on love") was recorded by Mallanaga Vātsyāyana, a philos-opher and scholar. The son of a Brahmin priest, he spent much time in the care of his favorite aunt at the brothel where she worked. Vātsyāyana, however, was celibate his whole life!

The *Kama Sutra* offers plenty of advice on kissing. For the gentlemen: "When you come home and she is sleeping, you should try to give her a kiss to rouse her, and rouse her well." And for the ladies: "At all times, when kissing and such like things are begun, the woman should give a reply with a hissing sound."

The *Kama Sutra* lists three

different types of kisses for young girls:

◆ the "nominal" kiss: when a girl touches the mouth of her lover with her own but doesn't do anything more

◆ the "throbbing" kiss: when a girl moves her lower lip but not her upper one

◆ the "touching" kiss: when a girl touches her lover's lips with her tongue and closes her eyes

There is also the "demonstrative" kiss where a man comes up to a woman and kisses her hand (or if she is seated, her toe!). And the kiss that we call the "French kiss," they called the "fighting of the tongue."

Although Vātsyāyana is credited with writing the text of the *Kama Sutra*, the content, according to myth, is courtesy of Nandi, the sacred bull of the god Shiva. Nandi was Shiva's doorkeeper. One night, he overheard Shiva making love to his wife and was so inspired that he gave "sacred utterance," which was later recorded for the benefit of mankind.

Greek Kisses

HER ARMS ABOUT HIS NECK, AND A WARM DEW
OF KISSES POURED UPON HIM, AND THUS SPAKE,
"FROWN NOT, ODYSSEUS, THOU ART WISE AND TRUE."

—Homer, *Odyssey*

hen Alexander the Great invaded India in 356 BC, he "discovered" spices, tea, and something that was hotter and spicier than both combined—kissing. His men brought the practice back to Greece where it caught on like wildfire (people knew a good thing when they saw it).

People kissed in greeting, but only according to their social status. Nobles were allowed to kiss each

∽ Mistletoe Myths ∾

The ancient Druids considered the mistletoe a sacred plant. It was hung over doorways to provide protection against thunder, lightning, and other evils. It was placed in babies' cradles to keep them from harm. Giving a sprig of mistletoe to the first cow that calved in the New Year could protect the entire herd for a year. But kissing under the mistletoe was not a Druid custom. That tradition came from Norse mythology.

The Norse god Balder was a favorite of the gods. His mother, Frigg, was the goddess of beauty and love. When Balder began having troubling dreams, his mother, a clairvoyant, realized this meant he was going to die. Frigg traveled the world, making every living thing promise not to harm her beloved son. She secured promises from the four elements: earth, fire, wind, and water. Balder was invincible, or so Frigg believed.

But Frigg had failed to get a promise from the mistletoe because she thought it was too young and too weak to harm Balder. Loki, the jealous trickster, discovered this and came up with a plan. He fashioned an arrow from the wood of the mistletoe and gave it to Balder's blind brother, Hod. Loki guided Hod's hand as he shot the arrow into the air and it found its way straight into Balder's heart.

The distraught Frigg cried a thousand tears, which became the mistletoe's white berries. Since Balder was the god of vegetation, winter came to the land, and much hardship followed. Eventually, the goddess of the underworld agreed to restore Balder to life. Frigg was grateful and declared that the mistletoe would bring love rather than death from that day forward. She hung up mistletoe everywhere, and promised to kiss anyone who passed underneath.

other's hands or cheeks; lower-ranking individuals had to kiss their superior's feet or the ground. Parents kissed children, sometimes with a *chutra* or "jug kiss," which was a bizarre practice of holding them up by the ears, as if they were the handles of a jug. Pericles, when returning from the marketplace twice a day, would greet his wife, Aspasia, with a tender kiss (even though it was seen as somewhat unmanly, at the time).

There were also male-on-male kisses. At Megara, the warrior Diocles, fell in love with a lad named

Philolaus. During a battle, Diocles protected his lover with his shield and was slain. A festival was held each year to honor Diocles, and included gymnastics, games, and a kissing contest. A laurel wreath was given to the boy who could kiss a male judge the longest.

Another myth told of Pygmalion, the king of Cyprus. Ovid recounted this in *Metamorphoses*. Pygmalion carved a statue of his ideal woman, Galatea. He fell in love with the statue and prayed to Aphrodite to bring it to life. Pygmalion was hopeful and "on the lips a burning kiss impress'd." What happened?

> *'Tis true, the harden'd Breast*
> *resists the Gripe,*
> *And the cold Lips return a Kiss*
> *unripe:*
> *But when, retiring back, he*
> *look'd again,*
> *To think it Iv'ry, was a thought*
> *too mean.* (25-8)

Encouraged, Pygmalion kissed Galatea again. This time:

> *He kisses her white Lips, renews*
> *the Bliss,*
> *And looks, and thinks they*
> *redden at the Kiss.* (75-6)

Finally, Galatea becomes human,

and Pygmalion is one happy man!

Then Lips to Lips he join'd; now
freed from Fear,
He found the Savor of the Kiss
sincere. (92-3)

Longus wrote a more light hearted romance about kissing in the second century AD. Two shepherd children named Daphnis and Chloe were raised together, and slowly realized they were falling in love. When Daphnis stole a kiss he wondered, "Whatever is Chloe's kiss doing to me? Her lips are softer than roses and her mouth is sweeter than honey, but her kiss hurts more than the sting of a bee" (18-20). Chloe's face suddenly dazzled him and he found himself shivering and blushing. "My breath's coming in gasps, my heart's jumping up and down, my soul's melting away—but all the same, I want to kiss her again. . . . Oh, what a strange disease—I don't even know what to call it" (23-28).

Kissing. What a strange disease, indeed.

Medieval Kisses

KISSING THINE EYES, THY RED LIPS SWEET
THAT MINE IN ONE LONG KISS SHOULD MEET.

—Pierre Vidal

 he knights of the Round Table; damsels in distress; chivalrous love; and bloody crusades. Ah, the middle ages.

Those who were illiterate would sign a contract with an X, and then kiss it to show sincerity; thus, the use of an X to symbolize a kiss today. Kissing was also a common greeting, and a sign of trust. After all, if you allowed someone close enough to kiss you, you trusted them not to stab you in the back.

If you want the daughter, you must kiss the mother. —Italian proverb

Knights would kiss their wives when they returned from the crusades. But it wasn't that they missed them! Women were forbidden to drink, so it was a way for knights to discover if their wives had been tapping into the mead barrels while they were away.

Dentistry not being what it is today, there was another practical use for a kiss. In Germany, the suggested cure for a cavity was to kiss a donkey (although, we hope, not necessarily on the mouth).

The troubadours are credited with giving us the modern love ballad. The morning song, "Alba," written anonymously, described the longing of a knight for his lady as they took leave of each other after a night of forbidden love.

Come let us kiss, dear lover, you and I,
Within the meads where pretty song-birds fly;
We will do all despite the jealous eye:
Ah God, ah God, the dawn!
It comes how soon. (9-12)

The image of a troubadour is often one of a lovesick ruffian playing a lute under a moonlit balcony, in an attempt to win his lady's hand. But this wasn't the case. More often than not, troubadours were rich, educated young men. And the "damsels" were usually married—albeit unhappily, since marriages were arranged. The songs were a form of entertainment, a far cry from the famines, plagues, and inquisitions of the day. Singing to a woman of noble birth was a way of advancing a troubadour's career. They were usually more interested in capturing the ladies' hearts and minds (and favors) than in getting them in bed.

Pierre Vidal was a notable exception. One of the most talented and prolific troubadours of his day, he was also, according to his biographer, "the maddest man in all the world." Erratic and reckless, his many escapades included posing as a swaggering knight, a landless outcast, and the emperor of Jerusalem! Vidal fell in love with Azalais, the wife of the Viscount Barral de Baux, and sneaked into her bedchamber to steal a kiss. But he was caught, and was forced to flee to Marseilles. Undaunted, Vidal continued to write songs of his love for the viscountess from there.

I entered her room and stole a
*   kiss from her on the mouth*
*   and chin.*
That is all that I had.
I am dead if she withholds the
*   rest.*

There was a smaller, more obscure group of female singers, known as the trobairitz. While their male counterparts often had ulterior motives for their flattering songs, those of the trobairitz are considered to be more honest, singing of kisses that evoked great longing and pain, like those in the following lyrics, written anonymously.

Fair, sweet lover, how will you
*   endure your great ache for*
*   me out on the salty sea,*
When nothing that exists could
*   ever tell the deep grief*
*   that has come into my heart?*
When I think of your gentle,
*   sparkling face that I used to*
*   kiss and caress,*
It is a great miracle that I am
*   not deranged. . . .*

One of the most famous love stories of the medieval period was that of Lancelot and Guinevere. Their love brought about the

❦ Eleventh Century Kissing ❧

In the eleventh century, Lady Murasaki Shikibu wrote *Tales of the Genji*. Often called the world's first novel, it described the libidinous lifestyle, which included lustful kissing that occurred in the courts of Japan.

Also in the eleventh century, in the Islamic world, Walladah bint al-Mustakfi was born into a powerful family. Her father was Mohammed III, the Caliph of Cordoba, Spain. When he died, having no male heirs, Walladah inherited his great fortune, allowing her to live as she pleased. She gave wild parties, had numerous lovers (but never married), and wrote poetry:

> *Forsooth, I allow my lover to*
> *touch my cheek,*
> *And bestow my kiss on him*
> *who craves it.*

Walladah is considered one of the most important female poets of her time. Little of her work survives, but we are fortunate to have those lines.

destruction of King Arthur's Round Table—and it all started with a kiss.

When Lancelot first came to court, he was stunned by the beauty of Arthur's wife, Guinevere. He became a great knight, and the noblest figure in the land. But his deeds weren't done out of devotion to the king. Instead, they were inspired by his love for Queen Guinevere.

Lancelot bemoaned the fact that Guinevere was married. Then his friend Galehaut discovered the reason for his distemper. But rather than being upset by the moral impropriety of it, Galehaut decided to help. He arranged a meeting between Guinevere and the so-called Black Knight who had saved her husband's life. (Lancelot did not want anyone to know his real name.) And he extracted a promise that she would kiss him as a token of her respect.

When Guinevere and Lancelot met, Galehaut used his body to block a view of them from the prying eyes of the court. The two shared their first kiss, which became much more than a token of respect. As William Morris later wrote:

*Came Lancelot walking; this is
    true, the kiss
Wherewith we kissed in meeting
    that spring day,
I scarce dare talk of the
    remember'd bliss. (132-34)*

But, alas, their love was doomed. Lancelot might have been one of the greatest knights in all the land, but owing to the impurity of his soul, he failed to secure the Holy Grail. And it was only a matter of time before the two lovers were caught. Lancelot escaped, but Guinevere was charged with treason and sentenced to be burned alive.

Just before the execution, Lancelot and his kinsmen charged to her rescue. In the resulting battle, many of King Arthur's most loyal knights were slain. In one version of the story, Guinevere went to a nunnery, and Lancelot and his followers broke away from King Arthur and formed a rival court in France. But peace was never restored to the country, and Camelot was never the same.

There were lighter stories about kissing, as well. The practice of locking lips had created much social anxiety; the line between platonic

✤ Religious Kissing ✤

Catholics sometimes kiss their rosary beads, and visitors to Rome will kiss the Pope's ring. The bronze statue of St. Peter, at the Vatican, has been kissed so many times that the toe of the right foot has been worn away.

The pope will kiss the ground when he arrives in a new country. In 1999, Pope John II bowed and kissed the Koran, as a sign of respect, after an Islamic delegation gave it to him as a gift.

But Christians are not the only ones to kiss holy relics. In the Jewish liturgy, the faithful will touch the Torah and then kiss their hand. They also kiss the Western wall of the temple in Jerusalem, which is their holiest site.

Hindus and Sikhs often kiss the ground of a temple. And Muslims kiss the black stone during their pilgrimage to Mecca, just as the prophet Mohammed once did.

kisses and sexual ones was often unclear. Chaucer parodied this in *The Canterbury Tales*. In "The Miller's Tale," Absalom asked Allison for a kiss, but she explained she was in love with another. Absalom persisted, so to finally get rid of him, Allison said that she would give him a kiss, but only if it was done in the dark. Absalom readily agreed. Only too late did he realize that it wasn't a good idea.

> *And Absalom no better felt nor worse*
> *But with his mouth he kissed her naked arse*
> *Right greedily, before he knew of this.*
> *Aback he leapt—it seemed somehow amiss.* (451-54)

Hmmm. . . . Maybe "air kisses" have their merits after all.

Renaissance Kisses

I UNDERSTAND THY KISSES, AND THOU MINE
AND THAT'S A FEELING DISPUTATION.

— William Shakespeare

During the Renaissance, poets elevated kissing to a more romantic, and erotic, plane. They used evocative sensory images, comparing it to honey, mead, sugar, and wine.

In *Basia* ("Kisses"), the Dutch poet Johannes Secundus tells of the sweetness of a kiss:

> 'Tis not a Kiss you give, my
>   Love!
> 'Tis richest nectar from above!
> A fragrant show'r of balmy dews,
> Which thy sweet lips alone

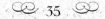

In love, there is always one who kisses and one who offers the cheek. —French proverb

diffuse! (1-4)

Ben Jonson compared kissing (most favorably) to wine:

Drink to me, only, with thine eyes
And I will pledge with mine;
Or leave a kiss but in the cup,
And I'll not look for wine. (1-4)

And in *Venus and Adonis*, Shakespeare suggestively wrote:

Graze on my lips; and if those hills be dry,
Stray lower, where the pleasant fountains lie. (233-34)

Some, like Daniel Heinsius, warned of the potent power of kissing: "You may conquer with the sword, But you are conquered with a kiss."

Others weren't so modest. The Persian poet Ha-fez worried of the effects his kisses would have on his love, that they would "char her delicate lips."

In England, Robert Herrick became known as the "Kissing Poet" because of the vast number of poems he wrote on the subject. Herrick was an ordained Episcopal deacon and remained a bachelor all of his life. His poems were addressed to a number of different women. But no one knows whether the women were real or a figment of his very fertile imagination.

But it is really Johannes Secundus who takes the "kissing cake." For what can compare to verses like these?

> *Whisper'd plaints, and wanton wiles;*
> *Speeches soft, and soothing smiles;*
> *Teeth-imprinted, tell-tale blisses;*
> *Intermix with all thy kisses. (1-4)*

Much like the ancient Egyptian myth when Isis kissed Osiris, the themes of transformation and rebirth echo over and over again.

One such story, which is similar to latter-day fairy tales, tells of an evil stepmother who changes a young maiden into a lime tree. The maid stood for ten years, pinned to the ground, until the king's son came along and kissed her roots.

> *King Magnus kisses the*
> *lime-tree's root*
> *From the kiss emerges two*
> *maiden feet*
> *King Magnus kisses the*
> *lime-tree's branch*
> *From the kiss emerges two*
> *maiden legs*
> *King Magnus kisses the*

⊰ Saint Valentine ⊱

Many believe Saint Valentine was a martyred priest who lived during the third century. ("Valentine" is derived from the word *valens*, which means worthy.) The emperor, Claudius, had outlawed marriage. Rome was involved in many bloody campaigns, and Claudius wanted to recruit young men as soldiers, rather than having them settle down.

According to legend, Valentine thought this unjust, and performed marriages in secret. One story also says he gave a gift of a flower from his garden, to all who visited him.

When Emperor Claudius learned Valentine was defying his "no marriage" rule, he was enraged. He had the priest arrested, and tried to force him to renounce his faith.

Valentine refused, and was imprisoned. He fell in love with the jailer's blind daughter, and miraculously restored her sight. Valentine was beheaded on February 14, 269 AD, but just before he died, he sent his love a farewell letter. He signed it, "From your Valentine."

lime-tree's leaf
It becomes a maiden, strange and
beautiful. (14-16)

Other kisses of revival were not as successful: in Shakespeare's *Romeo and Juliet*, the star-crossed Romeo said:

I dreamed my lady came and
found me dead,
And breathed such life with
kisses in my lips
That I revived, and was an
emperor. (5.6, 8-9)

But Romeo didn't revive, and he didn't become an emperor. Instead, Romeo gave his love a final farewell, when he said, "With this kiss, I die."

The idea of dying with a kiss was no less romantic than being revived by one. Poets borrowed from the ancient belief that you could catch the soul of a departed loved one on your lips, or at least keep it there a little longer.

With the abundance of love poetry, it is no wonder that during the Renaissance there was a whole lot of kissing going on! Nowhere was this truer than in jolly old England.

A kissing game was part of the festivities at country fairs. A maiden would give a clove-studded apple to a boy, who would bite off one of the cloves and give her a kiss. The boy would then take the apple, and go off to search for another maiden to kiss. By the time all the cloves were eaten, most everyone at the fair had been kissed once—if not twice! Before the days of mouthwash, the cloves served to sweeten the breath, and the apple cleaned the teeth.

Valentine's Day was also popular. This poem is from *Poor Robin's Almanac* (1757).

And, by the way, remember this
To seal the favor with a kiss.

This kiss begets more love, and
*   then*
That love begets a kiss again.

(9-12)

Upon entering a room, a gentleman was expected to kiss every woman present. And women would kiss anyone—and everyone—in sight. The visiting Dutch scholar Desiderius Erasmus of Rotterdam commented with delight: "English ladies are divinely pretty, and *too* good-natured. They have an excellent custom among them, that wherever you go the girls kiss you. They kiss you when you come, they kiss you when you go, they kiss you at intervening opportunities; their lips are soft, warm, and delicious."

But not everyone was happy about it. The French scholar Michel de Montaigne complained: "Kissing is a nauseous custom and injurious for the ladies, that they must be obliged to lend their lips to every fellow who has three footmen at his heels, however disgusting he may be in himself." Men didn't have it any easier, he argued. "For three beautiful women we must kiss threescore ugly ones."

But while England was known as a "country of kissers," Italy—the birthplace of the Renaissance and one of the most romantic countries in the world—was not. If a man embraced a woman in public, he could be forced to marry her. Not only that, but in 1562, a law was enacted in Naples that made kissing in public an offense that was punishable . . . by death.

Puritan Kisses

IF YOU KISS A WOMAN IN PUBLICK THOUGH OFFERED AS A COURTEOUS SALUTATION, IF ANY INFORMATION IS GIVEN TO THE SELECT MEMBERS, BOTH SHALL BE WHIPT OR FINED.

—Edward Ward (*Trip to New England*, 1699)

In 1620, Puritans immigrated to America and settled in the area that became known as New England. They felt the Church of England was too tolerant, and wanted to live in strict accordance with the Bible, free of any "distractions" that could lead to sin.

There were strict laws that governed every aspect of daily life. Wearing lace was not permitted, nor

Kissing is like drinking salted water. You drink, and your thirst increases. –Chinese proverb

 43

were playing cards, observing Christmas, drinking, blasphemy, or playing a musical instrument other than the harp, drum, or trumpet. The laws were voted on at town meetings, or in larger settlements, they were decided on by a group of Selectmen. Punishment was harsh for those who dared disobey these Selectmen.

There were also laws concerning kissing in public, and Captain Kemble, of Boston, found out the hard way. In 1656, Kemble returned home after three years at sea and greeted his wife with a kiss. But because it was the Sabbath, Kemble was charged with "lewd and unseemly behavior" and sentenced to two hours in the stocks!

In 1699, the Selectmen of Boston passed an ordinance that outlawed kissing in public altogether. It didn't last very long, but it made an impression on Edward Ward, a satirical writer who visited the city that same year.

Ward pointed out that if a man and a woman kissed in public, both could be whipped and fined. But there was an upside, he mockingly wrote:

It's an excellent Law to make Lovers in Private make much of their time, since open Lip-Lechery is so dearly purchased . . . and if they chance to be Detected, and are forc'd to pay the Fine, they are sure beforehand of something for their money.

But perhaps Ward was just waxing nostalgic, because "Old-England" was changing. And the practice of kissing was in freefall decline.

A major reason was the Great Plague, which devastated London in 1665, claiming one-fifth of the city's population—over 100,000 lives. All of a sudden, getting "up close and personal" didn't seem like such a good idea. Another reason was the increasing awareness of homosexuality. George Etherege paradied this in his play, *The Man of Mode*. "Lord, what a filthy trick these men have of kissing each other!" a woman selling oranges in the market remarked.

The play was a comedy, but the sentiment was not. Men who kissed other men—even in greeting—were looked upon as suspect. Writer

William Vaughan disparagingly wrote of ". . . the unnatural kiss of man with man, a minion-kiss, such as Jupiter used to Ganymede, his cup-bearer."

Ganymede was the young boy, in mythology, who caught Jupiter's eye and was brought to Mount Olympus to serve the gods. And a pamphlet was distributed on the streets of England with the following verse:

The world is chang'd, I know
not how
For men kiss men, not women
now;

A most unmanly, nasty trick
One man to lick the other's
cheek;
And only what renews the shame
Of J. the First, and Buckingham.

The anonymous pamphlet was referring to King James I and the Duke of Buckingham, who were known to be gay.

When it came to kissing, almost everyone was confused. In England, kissing had become a victim of its own success. Soon, kissing in public came to be viewed as highly inappropriate. Tipping hats, bowing, curtsying, and waving became the popular forms of greeting instead.

In other parts of Europe, the hand kiss became a popular form of greeting. It probably originated in the courts of Spain. Courtiers would pledge allegiance and show submission to those in authority by kissing their ring. It is no longer popular in most countries, but in Italy the *baciamano* ("hand kiss") is still used as a sign of respect, like in the ones given to Don Corleone in the movie *The Godfather*; or for kissing the pope's ring.

Victorian Kisses

ONCE HE DREW

WITH ONE LONG KISS, MY WHOLE SOUL THROUGH

MY LIPS, AS SUNLIGHT DRINKETH DEW.

—Alfred Tennyson

he Victorian era was a time of prudishness, repression, and restraint. These views were reinforced by people like Dr. William Acton who, in 1857, wrote: "The majority of women (happily for them) are not very much troubled with sexual feelings of any kind."

Young ladies were groomed for courtship and marriage from an early age; they were taught how to

Her kisses left something to be desired . . . the rest of her. –author unknown

 49

sew, read, play a musical instrument, and behave. A lady should refrain from all sexual contact before marriage. During courtship, she might permit a chaste kiss or a light squeeze of the hand; if a guy wanted to hold hands or put an arm around her waist, he'd better be prepared to "pop the question" first.

There were rules for men, too. When introduced to a lady, a man might "air-kiss" her hand, but he must wait for her to extend it, and never make the first move. A lady must *always* indicate that the kiss was welcome!

An actual hand kiss could occur if the two had been introduced before. For increasing degrees of familiarity, a delicate kiss on the forehead or (at most) the cheek was also allowed.

But there was one man who clearly hadn't read the memo. In 1837, kissing went to court when Thomas Saverland brought a lawsuit against Miss Caroline Newton. It seems he had tried to kiss her (apparently in jest), and she had responded . . . by biting off his nose!

The judge acquitted Miss

Newton, ruling that if a man kisses a woman against her will, "She is fully entitled to bite his nose, if she so pleases."

"And eat it up," a delighted barrister rejoined.

But still . . . there was romance. Lovers sent little gifts and hand-made cards on embossed paper, decorated with pictures, ribbons, and lace. One of these cards, which is preserved at the Strangers Hall Museum in Norwich, England, is dated and postmarked 1862. The card has a silver bird, surrounded by cherubs and flowers, and a printed message: "My dearest Miss, I send thee a kiss."

Three popular writers during the Victorian era were Currer, Acton, and Ellis Bell. Actually, they were the Brontë sisters (Charlotte, Anne, and Emily, respectively). Concerned about moral disapproval, and the prejudice of critics against women writers, they chose to write under gender-neutral pen names.

Charlotte Brontë's *Jane Eyre* is one of the best-known novels from this time. It tells the story of a governess who falls in love with her employer, Mr. Rochester:

❦ Revolutionary Kisses ❦

Napoleon Bonaparte and his wife, Josephine, were married in 1795. A few days later, Napoleon had to leave, in order to command the French army in Italy. From there, he wrote feverish love letters to Josephine.

He pleaded to Josephine to join him in Milan for a belated honeymoon:

Soon, I hope, I will be holding you in my arms; then I will cover you with a million hot kisses, burning like the equator.

He wrote to her passionately:

Kisses on your mouth, your eyes, your breast, everywhere, everywhere.

And evocatively:

A kiss on the heart and one lower down, much lower!

Go figure! One of the greatest military generals in history was actually quite a romantic at heart!

My love has sworn, with sealing kiss,
With me to live—to die;
I have at last my nameless bliss.
As I love—loved am I! (45-48)

There were real-life romances, as well. One of the greatest love stories is that of two poets: Elizabeth Barrett and Robert Browning. And it began in a most audacious way.

In 1844, Elizabeth Barrett was already a well-loved and respected poet in England. (She's best remembered for "How do I love thee, let me count the ways.")

But Elizabeth suffered more than her share of tragedies. She was afflicted by a lung ailment as a child (and used morphine for it the rest of her life). A serious fall injured her spinal cord when she was fifteen, leaving her a semi-invalid. Then her beloved brother, who accompanied her to the seaside to recuperate after the accident, drowned in a sailing accident.

Elizabeth lived with her tyrannical father, who objected to the marriage of any of his twelve children. He threatened to disown them if they were to disobey. A virtual prisoner in her father's home, Elizabeth became a recluse, spending most of her time alone in her bedroom where she continued to write.

Robert Browning, himself a young poet, read Elizabeth's work, and was so inspired that he decided to write to her.

The two met several times, and decided to marry, in secret, in 1846. When Elizabeth's father found out, true to his word, he disowned her, refusing to see her again, or open any of the letters she wrote.

The couple moved to Italy. Elizabeth's health improved, and she gave birth to a son. From there, both poets produced some of their most acclaimed works.

In *A Gondola*, Robert Browning described two lovers who stole away in Venice:

The moth's kiss, first!
Kiss me as if you made me
    believe
You were not sure, this eve,
How my face, your flower, had
    pursed
Its petals up; so, here and there
You brush it, till I grow aware
Who wants me, and wide open I
    burst.   (1-7)

And revising the age-old theme of a spiritual kiss, he penned these beautiful lines: "What of soul was left, I wonder, when the kissing had to stop?" Elizabeth echoed this when she revealed what her husband's love meant to her:

My own Beloved, who hast lifted me
From this drear flat of earth where I was thrown,
And, in betwixt the languid ringlets, blown
A life-breath, till the forehead hopefully
Shines out again, as all the angels see,
Before thy saving kiss!   *(1-7)*

Elizabeth died on June 29, 1861, in Italy. The love story that started with a letter, ended with a kiss; for as Robert held his wife in his arms, he later wrote, "Kissing me with such vehemence that when I laid her down she continued to kiss the air with her lips. . . ." Robert asked Elizabeth how she felt. "Beautiful," she replied.

The Early 1900s

I WONDER WHO'S KISSING HER NOW,
I WONDER WHO'S TEACHING HER NOW,
WONDER WHO'S LOOKING INTO HER EYES
BREATHING SIGHS, TELLING LIES.

—lyrics by Will M. Hough and Frank R. Adams (1909)

 e've made it into the twentieth century! Kissing has come along for a very bumpy ride—and it's not in for smooth sailing anytime soon.

In 1901, Danish philosopher Christopher Nyrop traced the origins of kissing to primitive senses of taste and smell.

Who kisses the feet of his mother, kisses the step of Paradise. —Turkish proverb

As to the age-old question—what do women want?—Nyrop (at least when it came to sensory kissing) thought he knew. "A kiss should not be too wet around the mouth," he wrote; girls were known to "scorn a kiss with sauce." The "tone color" is also important. It should be clear and ringing, not one that "sounded like when a cow drags her foot out of the swamp." Another tip: a beard and a moustache will make the girls swoon!

"Kissing a man without a beard is like kissing an egg without salt" is an old Danish proverb. Nyrop gives an "updated" version that was popular among refined young ladies of the day. "Kissing a fellow without a quid of tobacco and a beard is like kissing a clay wall." (Less-refined women put it a less-refined way: "Kissing one who neither smokes nor chews tobacco is like kissing a newborn calf on the rump.")

A few years later, Freud offered a more, well, Freudian view. He felt kissing was an "unconscious repetition of infantile delight in feeding"—a return to the mother's breast.

Freud was baffled by what he called "contact between the

mucous membranes of the lips . . . [which was] held in high sexual esteem among many nations in spite of the fact that the parts of the body involved do not form any part of the sexual apparatus but constitute the entrance to the digestive tract."

A group of men in Kansas obviously agreed! They formed the Anti-Kissing League, vowing never to kiss their wives (or girlfriends) again. They felt it was immoral, unhygienic, and could lead to fatal disease! There is no evidence of when the league disbanded (or if anyone cheated!), but one thing is certain: it couldn't have lasted very long!

On the other hand, kisses took on a sweet new meaning, when, in 1907, a little chocolate treat, shaped like a teardrop and wrapped in silver foil, appeared on store shelves for the very first time. That's right—Hershey's Kisses! Kissing was becoming a popular commodity—a far cry from the ancient and spiritual kisses of yore.

Another thing that was having an influence on kissing? Movies! And they've been having an influence ever since. Silent films were shown in town halls and theaters everywhere. They had on-screen titles in lieu of dialogue and narration, and were accompanied by mood-setting music that was often improvised.

After the notoriety (and success) of *The Kiss* in 1898, producers quickly realized that a good lip-lock could spell instant success. A whole crop of films premiered, with titles like *The Kiss of Mary Jane* (1911); *The Elusive Kiss* (1913); *The Germ in the Kiss* (1914); *The Five Hundred Dollar Kiss* (1914); and (for the budget-minded), *Fifty Dollars for a Kiss* (1915). There was *The Kiss of Death*

(1915); *Kiss of Hate* (1916); *Kiss for Suzie* (1917); and *The Enchanted Kiss* (1917); and the intriguingly titled *A High Diver's Last Kiss* (1918). In all, there were over two dozen titles containing the word "kiss."

There was also the cinema's first (*almost*) homosexual kiss.

In Charlie Chaplin's movie *Behind the Screen (1916)*, Chaplin played an over-worked prop man, who fell in love with an unemployed actress. She decided to cross-dress in order to get a job as a stagehand. When the burly foreman, Goliath, discovered her and Chaplin kissing, he berated them for being gay.

But while men and women everywhere were kissing, toasting, and raising their glasses in song, something else was going on. In 1914, World War I broke out.

Many of the love songs were sad and sentimental. One of the most popular was called "Till We Meet Again," and told of a soldier leaving his sweetheart, as he went off to war.

Smile the while you kiss me sad
*   adieu*
When the clouds roll by I'll come
*   to you*
Then the skies will seem more
*   blue*
Down in Lover's Lane, my
*   dearie. (5-8)*

Soldiers who were stationed in France sent kisses back home. Embroidered silk postcards could be purchased in small shops in the army camps. These lovely little cards were decorated with bright, embroidered flowers and cheery words of greeting—often "Kisses from France."

The Roaring Twenties

I WASN'T KISSING HER, I WAS WHISPERING IN HER MOUTH.

—Chico Marx (to his wife, when she caught him kissing a showgirl)

he "Roaring Twenties" were a time of flapper girls, jazz, and bootlegged gin. Colleges were going co-ed, and the Ford Model T was increasingly popular. Backseat make-out sessions, petting, and premarital sex were becoming the new norm.

And then, there were prudes. Henry Stanton wrote a self-help book in 1922 called *Sex: Avoided Subjects Discussed in Plain English*. He warned that physical intimacy before marriage could lead to one's moral downfall—or worse!

The holding of hands and similar

innocent beginnings often pave the way for more familiar caresses. Passionate kisses—the promiscuous kiss, by the way, may be the carrier of that dread infection, syphilis—violently awaken a young girl's sex instincts.

It was the golden age of silent film, with actors like Marlene Dietrich, Clara Bow, Greta Garbo, Gloria Swanson, John Barrymore, and Douglas Fairbanks heating up the screen.

One of the biggest heartthrobs was Rudolph Valentino (a.k.a. the "Latin Lover" to scores of adoring fans). Valentino's big break came in the role of a playboy in *The Four Horsemen of the Apocalypse*. The climax was a sexy tango and a steamy kiss in a smoke-filled Argentina café.

Valentino starred in thirty-seven movies, playing an Arabian sheik, a hot-blooded matador, and a notorious ladies' man. His movies were replete with kisses—including "hand kisses" that were executed with such perfection, they seemed downright chic and debonair.

Gloria Swanson starred with Valentino in *Beyond the Rocks* in

1922. In her autobiography, *Swanson on Swanson*, she recounted early America censorship rules that tried to control the heat on the screen.

> *We shot each kiss twice, once for the version to be released in America and one for the European version. Only Europeans and South Americans could see Swanson and Valentino engage in any honest-to-goodness torrid kisses. American fevers were now controlled by a stopwatch.*

The rules stemmed from a 1915 Supreme Court ruling, stating that movie-making was a business rather than an art, and wasn't protected by the First Amendment. The motion picture industry hired Will H. Hays, to act as censorship "czar," who issued a list of rules. Compliance was mainly voluntary, but it created problems, nonetheless.

Perhaps it was because the movies were a new art/business form, but there were many record-setting kisses during the "roaring twenties."

American and Chinese moviemakers weren't the only ones jumping on the kissing bandwagon. From Egypt, there was *Kubla fil*

∼ Kissing Superlatives ∼

FIRST DOCUMENTARY/ NOSE-KISS

Nanook of the North (1922) The first feature-length documentary was filmed in the Canadian Arctic and introduced viewers to the traditional Inuit way of life. But what really captured the audience's imagination was when Nanook and his wife nose-kissed. Most had never heard of this sensual delight! The movie created a nose-kissing frenzy and started a trend among amorous teens.

FIRST LESBIAN KISS

Manslaughter (1922) Cecil B. De-Mille's movie featured a scene of the de-bauchery in ancient Rome, including an orgy and the first female-female kiss.

MOST KISSES IN A SINGLE MOVIE

Don Juan (1926)   The movie was two hours and forty-seven minutes long, during which John Barrymore (as Juan) planted a kiss on a woman 191 times. That's one kiss every fifty-three seconds—as studio heads pointed out in their advertising campaign.

FIRST CHINESE MOVIE TO SHOW KISSING

Two Women in the House (1926)

Kissing became common in Chinese movies, right up until the founding of the People's Republic of China, in 1949, after which it nearly disappeared.

FIRST OPEN-MOUTHED KISS

Flesh and the Devil (1926) Real-life lovers Greta Garbo and John Gilbert smooched. Not only that, but the kiss was horizontal, and Garbo was the aggressor!

FIRST MALE-ON-MALE KISS

Wings (1927) A fighter pilot, during World War I gives a parting kiss to his dying friend. The Oscars were introduced that year, and *Wings* won the first Best Picture award. It is the only silent film ever to win.

Sahara (*A Kiss in the Desert*); from India, *Ekaj Chumban* (*Fatal Kiss*); from France, *Embrassez-moi* (*Kiss Me*); and from Germany *Ich küsse ihre Hand, Madame* (*I Kiss Your Hand, Madam*).

In 1929, Greta Garbo appeared in the last film MGM made without dialogue—*The Kiss*. It was the end of the silent film era, but not of screen kisses. With the advent of the "talkies" more sweet, scandalous kisses were about to unfold.

The Thirties and Forties

I MARRIED THE FIRST MAN I EVER KISSED.
WHEN I TELL MY CHILDREN THAT, THEY JUST ABOUT THROW UP.

—Former First Lady Barbara Bush

n 1936, William Morris wrote *The Art of Kissing*, a book with a unique—and delicious—point of view. It's a how-to manual, with sections like "How to Approach a Girl," "Preparing for a Kiss," and "How to Kiss Girls with Different Sizes of Mouths."

Variety is really the spice of life, and Morris described a whole pot-pourri of kisses that are sure to

A kiss without a hug is like a flower without fragrance. —Maltese proverb

make the girls swoon. There's the "Vacuum Kiss" ("suck inward as though you were trying to draw out the innards of an orange"), the "Nip Kiss" (leave your lips open "as though you were going to nibble on a delicious tidbit"), and the "Electric Kiss" (turn off the lights, "shuffle about on the carpet until they are charged with electricity . . . kiss in the dark and make the sparks fly").

But what about the "Perfect Kiss"? Not to worry—Morris gives plenty of advice on how to execute that!

Like a sea-gull swooping gracefully down through the air, bring your lips down firmly onto the lips of the girl who is quivering in your arms.

Swooping and quivering and sparks . . . oh my! Morris must have been watching too many movies. At least, before the new censorship rules kicked in.

William H. Hays had been working on cleaning up Hollywood since 1921, and in 1930, a Catholic priest named Daniel A. Lord contacted him. Lord was perturbed by the lack of "morality and decency" in the movies. "Silent smut had been bad. Vocal smut cried to the censors for vengeance," he would later write.

Lord created a code of ethics, based on the Ten Commandments, which would serve as a moral compass for Hollywood. Lord's document, with only a few minor changes, would go on to be implemented by Hays' office and called the Production (Hays) Code. It banned the portrayal of illegal drug use, nudity, sex, profanity, and anyone profiting from gambling and crime. It also stated:

Excessive and lustful kissing, lustful embraces, suggestive postures and gestures, are not to be shown.

What constituted "excessive and lustful" kissing was open to interpretation; but even Woody Woodpecker had to tow the line. A girl could kiss Woody, and he could kiss another animal, but he couldn't kiss a human being (even if it was an animated one).

Still, for the first few years of its existence, the Production Code was only haphazardly enforced. It might have stayed that way, too—but then along came a former vaudeville

☙ Kissing Superlatives ☜

FIRST (DISGUISED) FEMALE-FEMALE KISS
Morocco (1930) Marlene Dietrich, dressed in a top hat and tails, kisses a young lady in a cabaret.

FIRST HINDI KISS
Karma (1933) Devika Rani and her real-life husband, Himanshu Rai, kiss.

FIRST DRIVE-IN MOVIE OPENS
(1933) No record of the first kiss here, but there were probably plenty—both on and *off* the screen.

FIRST FULL-LENGTH ANIMATED FEATURE
Snow White (1937) Snow White is awakened by a kiss, and kisses the dwarfs goodbye before she and the prince ride off together at the end.

LONGEST KISS IN THE FILM
You're in the Army Now (1941) Regis Toomey's kiss with Jane Wyman is three minutes and five seconds long.

performer who was so brash and sassy, she caused the ears of the religious right to burn!

Mae West wrote and acted in her own movies, which were replete with steamy sexuality, innuendos, and quips. "Is that a pistol in your pocket, or are you glad to see me?" was one of her most memorable lines.

Mae West has often been given the "distinction" of being almost single-handedly responsible for the tightening of the censorship screws! Her movies incensed religious conservatives, the Catholic church threatened massive boycotts, and right-wing financiers threatened to "pull the plug" on all of Hollywood. So, in 1934, the Production Code began to be strictly enforced, and remained in effect for the next twenty-five years.

Mae West continued to butt heads with censors for the rest of her career. She became master of the double entendre in order to escape the censor's notice.

West appeared on a popular radio show, *The Chase and Sanborn Hour*, along with ventriloquist Edgar Bergen. She bantered with the dummy, Charlie McCarthy, about the previous night they had supposedly spent together. "You're all wood and a yard long," West saucily complained; and his kisses gave her splinters. She was subsequently banned from NBC for life!

While Mae West was entertaining fans and enraging critics —often at the same time!—other kisses managed to squeak past the censors and onto the big screen. In *Gone with the Wind* (1939), Rhett Butler (Clark Gable) told Scarlett O'Hara (Vivien Leigh) that he loved her and wanted her arms wrapped around him, and then asked her to kiss him. He then went on to tell her she should be kissed often, and by someone who knows how.

Despite being in perhaps the most famous movie in history, Vivien Leigh didn't want Clark Gable to kiss her. It is rumored that Clark Gable had such bad halitosis, she didn't want to be kissed by him *at all!*

In 1946, Alfred Hitchcock's movie *Notorious* featured a legendary kissing scene between Ingrid Bergman and Cary Grant. Hitchcock slyly circumvented the

Kissing Quotes

"Any man who can drive safely while kissing a pretty girl is simply not giving the kiss the attention it deserves."
—Albert Einstein

"A kiss is a lovely trick designed by nature to stop speech when words become superfluous."
—Ingrid Bergman

"A man snatches the first kiss, pleads for the second, demands the third, takes the fourth, accepts the fifth—and endures all the rest."
—Helen Rowland

"People who throw kisses are hopelessly lazy."
—Bob Hope

"The first kiss is stolen by the man; the last is begged by the woman."
—Henry Louis Mencken

censorship rules that stated a kiss could be no more than three seconds long. He had the actors' lips touch for three seconds, then pull away, and then touch again and again and *again*! The entire sizzling sequence was 180 seconds long!

Then there was *Casablanca (1942)*. The scene was set: It was nighttime in Paris. Rick (Humphrey Bogart) poured Ilsa (Ingrid Bergman) a glass of champagne. They kissed, and Ilsa asked Rick to kiss her as if there would never be another.

Judy Garland was known not only for her acting (most notably as Dorothy in *The Wizard of Oz*, where she kissed the Straw Man, the Tin Man, and the Cowardly Lion goodbye), but for her beautiful poetry, some about kissing.

Meanwhile, another favorite actress, Shirley Temple, was growing up. In 1945, she starred in the movie *Kiss and Tell*, and as part of the publicity, she spread some cheer to some soldiers at a charity kissing booth.

Two years later, in *The Hagen Girl*, the star got her first screen kiss—from Ronald Reagan. Reagan was reluctant; he was sixteen years older, and argued his character should end up kissing the school-teacher, instead.

The kiss went over like a lead balloon—and not just because of the difference in age. Audiences found it hard to accept that instead of singing "On the Good Ship, Lollipop," their dear little Shirley was locking lips onscreen.

During this period, Duke Ellington composed "Prelude to a Kiss." Ingrid Bergman said to Gary Cooper (*For Whom the Bell Tolls*), she didn't know how to kiss or where the noses go. And a truly iconic image became one of the most famous photographs in kisstory.

On August 14, 1945—the day that marked the end of World War II—Alfred Eisenstaedt took a picture of a sailor kissing a woman in Times Square. It looked as if the sailor took a page from William Morris' playbook, gracefully swooping down over the woman, and holding her so that her torso was almost parallel to the ground. It wasn't a passionate reunion, however; the soldier was drunk, and in joyous celebration, was serial-smooching every woman who walked by!

The 1950s

HOLLYWOOD IS A PLACE WHERE THEY'LL PAY YOU
A THOUSAND DOLLARS FOR A KISS, AND FIFTY CENTS FOR YOUR SOUL.

— Marilyn Monroe

The fifties started off with a warning. Bacteriologist Arthur Bryand, at the Baltimore City College in Maryland, found that up to 250 colonies of bacteria could be transferred with a single kiss!

But kissing was on a roll—and neither censorship, nor health warnings, could dampen the mood. It was still a favorite topic in music and in art; plus, there was a new media darling—TV. People gathered around their big clunky sets, adjusted the rabbit ears, ate prepackaged frozen dinners on little aluminum trays, and watched kisses that were of the "family-friendly" kind.

The Ed Sullivan Show featured Topo Gigio, the puppet mouse, who delighted audiences when he asked Ed to kiss him goodnight. The dour host would lose his scowl (at least, for a moment) to give the cheeky little mouse a peck on the cheek!

Then there was *I Love Lucy*, the popular black and white sitcom starring Lucille Ball and Desi Arnaz. The two shared greeting kisses and goodnight kisses, and

Ricky sang about kissing Lucy.

Each episode—after Lucy's hilarious antics landed her in trouble with Ricky—there was a "make-up kiss" at the end of the show. Still, *I Love Lucy* managed to get into hot water with the censors. Because Lucy and Desi were married in real life, they were the only couple allowed to be shown in the bedroom together—albeit in single beds, and with at least one person having one foot firmly planted on the floor!

In one episode, Lucy was in her (single) bed, and dressed in a flannel nightgown. Ricky came in and planted a serious smooch on her lips that was over seven seconds long! The kiss made it past the censor the first time around, but was drastically cut for subsequent reruns.

Of course, smooching was still a reason to break out in song. *Kisses Sweeter Than Wine*, written by the Weavers, became a hit for both Jimmy Rodgers and Frankie Vaughn. Jazz great Louis Armstrong sang "A Kiss to Build a Dream On."

One song was so controversial that it was banned by the Roman Catholic church in Boston. It was called "I Saw Mommy Kissing Santa Claus!" It was released by Columbia Records in 1952, and featured the young Jimmy Boyd, who was all of twelve years and eleven months old. The song rocketed Jimmy to stardom and became number one on the Billboard Charts. So what could religious leaders possibly object to? Apparently, the song mixed Christmas—with sex!

Then there was Elvis! With his gyrating hips, smooth vocal cords, and rhinestone-studded jumpsuits, he blasted onto the kissing scene.

So provocative was "The King" that when he appeared on *The Ed Sullivan Show*, he was censored, and only shown from the waist up.

Elvis' songs were sometimes sweet, and other times borderline silly. Bernard Weinman and Lee Rosenberg topped the charts in 1957 with their song about kissing, "Too Much."

They kissed girls in the audience, and those that jumped up onstage with them. For girls not lucky enough to push through the screaming mobs, there were fan magazines. *16 Magazine* debuted with a photo of a smiling, waving Elvis on the cover—and flew off the shelves. One can only imagine legions of lovesick teens pinning photos on their walls, and kissing Elvis goodnight!

Then, there was Elvis' love scene in the movie *Jailhouse Rock*. Jennifer (Sherry Wilson) lay on a couch while Elvis kissed her.

In 1958, the musical *Bye Bye Birdie* appeared on Broadway and became an instant hit. It centered on Conrad Birdie, a rock-and-roll singer who had been conscripted into the army. It was based on Elvis, who had just

Kissing Marilyn

In the movie, *Some Like it Hot* (1959), Tony Curtis played Joe/Josephine, a struggling musician who witnessed a mob hit, and disguised himself as a member of a female rock band. He fell for Sugar (Marilyn Monroe).

People were outraged, though, when Curtis said kissing Marilyn was like "kissing Hitler." He later set the record straight, in his autobiography *An American Prince*. After a steamy scene on a yacht, some of the crew were standing around, watching the rushes, and asked him what it was like to kiss the blonde bombshell. Curtis thought that such a stupid question deserved an equally stupid answer.

"I flippantly responded by saying, 'Kissing Marilyn is like kissing Hitler.' I was right—it was a stupid answer. What I should have said was, 'What do you think kissing her is like, birdbrain?' "

been conscripted that year.

In the play, a publicity gimmick was created. Birdie was to sing a new song called "One Last Kiss" on *The Ed Sullivan Show*, and then plant a kiss on one lucky girl in the audience.

The show was a satire of life in the fifties, as when two teeny-boppers spread some gossip on the phone, and they sang about kissing.

There were also some memorable moments in the movies. In *From Here to Eternity* (1953), when Deborah Kerr and Burt Lancaster kissed on a deserted Hawaiian beach, it wasn't just the location that was sizzling hot! The sand, the waves splashing over their bodies, and the fact that Kerr played an adulterous army wife, added up to one unforgettable lip-lock.

East of Eden (1955) isn't memorable so much for its on-screen kiss as for a curious exchange that went on before filming even began. James Dean had already been cast in the lead role, and a relatively unknown actor came in to audition for the role of Dean's older brother. His name? Paul Newman, who was hoping for his big break.

For some reason, during the screen test, Dean decided to throw a curveball and ad-lib. The obviously flustered Newman didn't get the part! (It went to Raymond Massey, instead.)

In *Pillow Talk* (1959), Jan Morrow (Doris Day) began to worry when the man she was dating, Rex Stetson (Rock Hudson), never kissed her, and she worried he might be homosexual. When Rex commented about recipes, colors, fabrics, and their "friendship," Jan was flustered. She asked him if they were just friends or more, and Rex told her that her question deserved a "direct answer." Then he gave her a kiss—and a sensational one, at that!

The 1960s

**ALWAYS REMEMBER THIS: A KISS WILL NEVER MISS, AND
AFTER MANY KISSES A MISS BECOMES A MISSES.**

—John Lennon

The sixties were a time of peace, love, and rock-and-roll. Over seventy million baby boomers had become teens, and being young and hip was definitely where it was at. "Don't trust anyone over thirty" meant that old conservative views were out, replaced by the Civil Rights movement, "love ins," and anti-war protests. Guys grew their hair long and wore love beads; girls wore miniskirts, flowers in their hair, and hot pants.

A sponge to wipe away the past; a rose to sweeten the present; a kiss to greet the future. –Arabian proverb

There was Paul Anka, Gladys Knight and the Pips, the Supremes, Joni Mitchell, and Bob Dylan. Elvis returned from the army with a slew of postwar movies and songs. The Beach Boys sang "Kiss Me Baby," and Barbra Streisand sang "Kiss Me in the Rain." And The Beatles created mass hysteria among teenage girls with lyrics about kissing in "All My Lovin'."

In American cinema, the changing moral standards of the sixties, along with the influx of foreign movies (and their more explicit sexual content), meant that the Production Code was becoming irrelevant, and was often altogether ignored. There were many memorable movie kisses as a result.

In *Breakfast at Tiffany's*, Holly Golightly (Audrey Hepburn) and her boyfriend shared a passionate kiss in the pouring rain. In *The Graduate*, there is a smoking hot kiss—literally! Dustin Hoffman planted a good one on the cigarette-smoking Mrs. Robinson (Anne Bancroft) before she could exhale. In *Who's Afraid of Virginia Woolf*, the alcoholic Martha (Elizabeth Taylor) told her husband, George (Richard

Burton), to give her "a big sloppy kiss."

One of Andy Warhol's first films, *Kiss*, was fifty-four minutes long, and consisted entirely of scenes of couples kissing, each about three minutes in length.

But while American movies became more explicit, there was still a barrier to be broken—the first interracial kiss. That came in *Guess Who's Coming to Dinner* (1967), starring Sidney Poitier and Katherine Houghton as a young, engaged couple in love. There was only one kiss in the movie—and it was shown in the rearview mirror of a cab. Still, it was ground-breaking; while the movie was being filmed, interracial marriage was still unlawful in sixteen states. A Supreme Court ruling struck down those laws as unconstitutional shortly before the movie's release, but it resonated deeply when a detractor told the couple, "You'll be illegal in some states."

That same year, *Movin' with Nancy,* a musical special featuring Nancy Sinatra, aired on TV. After a rendition of the upbeat song, "What'd I Say," Nancy and Sammy

Davis Jr. kissed. But it took a little scheming on the stars' parts. The segment was filmed just before Davis had to leave for another job, so there was no way a retake could be done.

In 1968, the TV show *Star Trek* portrayed what has often been cited as TV's first interracial kiss. Although not accurate (it followed the Sinatra/Davis kiss), it was the first one in a drama, between actors playing a part—and the first truly delicious one, at that!

The kiss was between Captain Kirk (William Shatner) and Communications Officer Uhuru (Nichelle Nichols). When it came time to shoot the scene, it went off without a hitch. Then NBC officials, who were worried about angering conservative viewers in the deep south, ordered a second "kiss-less" version to be shot. Shatner objected to the censorship and purposely sabotaged subsequent takes, by looking into the camera and rolling his eyes. Network executives had little choice but to air the kiss, and were surprised when it received a unanimous thumbs-up.

By the time Woodstock rolled around, kissing had gone main-

Kiss of Death

During the mid-sixties, there was a "kiss of death"—this one courtesy of the KGB. That's what the little weapon disguised as a tube of lipstick was called. "The Lipstick Pistol" was used during the Cold War, and could fire a single 4.5 mm shot. One is on display at the International Spy Museum in Washington, D.C.

This wasn't the first "lipstick of death." Cleopatra used a plant called fucus as a dye in her lipstick, which made her lips look luscious but contained poisonous mercury. It's a good thing mouth kissing wasn't in vogue in ancient Egypt. Who knows how many would have perished from her charms!

stream. So when Jimi Hendrix took the stage at the festival, and sang about kissing the sky in "Purple Haze," nobody knew exactly what it meant—but they did know kissing was here to stay.

The 1970s

WE WERE PRETTY MUCH ALL ALONE OUT THERE,

AND IT WAS DARK AND COLD AND LATE. I KISSED HER AGAIN.

BUT NOT ON THE FOREHEAD, AND NOT LIGHTLY.

WHEN WE STOPPED KISSING, SHE WAS STILL HOLDING ONTO MY SLEEVE.

—Erich Segal (*Love Story*, 1970)

hew! We've made it past Woodstock, and the kiss has survived. It's been battered and bruised, but (to quote the popular 1970s band, the Bee Gees) it was definitely "stayin' alive."

This was a time of lava lamps, disco balls, and bell-bottom jeans. John Lennon sang "Kiss, Kiss, Kiss";

Better a slap from a wise man than a kiss from a fool. – Yiddish proverb

Bobby Vinton gave us "Sealed with a Kiss"; and from the Bee Gees came "Kiss of Life" and dozens of other very danceable tunes.

The band KISS appeared on the scene, shocking and rocking with their painted faces, names like Starchild, Spaceman, The Demon, and Catman, and stage performances that included pyrotechnics, fire-breathing, and smoking guitars.

Lipographs were invented in 1979 by David Bowie when he made a lipstick print of his kiss on a thank-you card. A publicist liked the idea and got Bowie, Mick Jagger, Jack Nicholson, Sean Connery, Sophia Loren, and other famous stars to make lipographs that were auctioned off at Sotheby's, in London. They raised $16,000 for the Save the Children Fund.

On TV, Marcia kissed heartthrob Davie Jones, in *The Brady Bunch* (even though it was on the cheek), and Charlie shared a magical moment with the Little Red-Haired Girl in *It's Your First Kiss, Charlie Brown* (but couldn't remember it the next day).

All in the Family, with the outspoken and narrow-minded

Archie Bunker (Carroll O'Connor) and his ditzy but lovable wife, Edith (Jean Stapleton), broke new ground by dealing with controversial issues of the day. In one famous episode, the subject turned to interracial kissing, when Sammy Davis Jr. made a guest appearance (as himself).

In the episode, Archie was working as a taxi driver and Davis visited his house to pick up a briefcase he left behind in the cab. Archie mentioned having seen the star on *The Johnny Carson Show,* and Edith piped up how Archie said he never thought he'd ever see "whites and coloreds" kissing and hugging. Archie tried to backtrack, but to no avail. It was clear he was a bigot through and through.

The highlight of the episode, though, came when Sammy Davis Jr. posed for a picture with Archie just before he left. At the very moment that the camera flashed, the star turned and planted a big, fat kiss on the stunned Archie's cheek! The audience's laughter went on for so long, it had to be edited to fit the timeframe for TV.

In the movies, there were first kisses (*Rocky*), last kisses (*Love*

∼✷ The Greeting Kiss ✷∼

In 1979, in *Miss Manners' Guide to Excruciatingly Correct Behavior,* Miss Manners (a.k.a. Judith Martin) said, "There is a great deal of kissing going on these days among people who do not especially like one another." She wasn't talking about romantic liplocks but "social kissing, an activity common among consenting, if unenthusiastic, adults." And she was right; there was a lot of it going on.

The new trend grew out of the openness of the sixties. As a result, there was "an inflation of intimate signals," University of California sociologist Murray Davis observed. "We kiss people we used to hug, hug people we used to shake hands with, and shake hands with people we used to nod to."

According to Miss Manners, acceptable places for a social kiss were the lips, the right check only, the right cheek followed by the left cheek, or the hand. "The consequences of kissing improperly range from having one's cheek hanging jilted in midair, to getting one's lips neatly severed by a diamond ring," she said. And "Cheek kissing in this country requires a minimum of one lady, but the partner may be either a lady or a gentleman."

Notice Miss Manners said "in this country," because the greeting kiss varies throughout the world. Germany is a no-kiss country, except between family members and very close friends. Those in Britain are also normally reserved. Belgians use one kiss for someone approximately their own age, and three for someone older. But the person must be at least ten years older. So unless you want to send someone for Botox, kisser beware!

Story), and adulterous kisses (Chinatown). There was also the "kiss of death"—Mafia style. In The Godfather, Michael Corleone (Al Pacino) approached his traitorous brother at a New Year's Eve party and whispered in his ear that a plane was waiting to take them to Miami. Then he gave his brother a truly lethal omen—a kiss on the lips!

The 1980s

SINCE THE INVENTION OF THE KISS THERE HAVE BEEN
FIVE KISSES THAT WERE RATED THE MOST PASSIONATE, THE MOST PURE.
THIS ONE LEFT THEM ALL BEHIND.

—*The Princess Bride* (1973)

 emember the eighties? There was breakdancing, Teenage Mutant Ninja Turtles, and Cabbage Patch Kids, along with Jane Fonda aerobics, and video games like Nintendo and Pac Man. On TV, a little-known talk show host named Oprah Winfrey dispensed her down-to-earth wisdom for the first time.

Another popular show, *The Golden Girls*, featured four older

The most eloquent silence . . . that of two mouths meeting in a kiss. –author unknown

women who became roommates. In one memorable moment the promiscuous Blanche (Rue McClanahan) told Dorothy (Bea Arthur) that she loved the rain because it reminded her of her first kiss. When Dorothy asked her if her first kiss was in the rain, Blanche told her "no"—it was in the shower!

The show *Cheers* took place in a neighborhood Boston bar. There was a lot of smooching between bartender Sam Malone (Ted Danson) and his co-worker Dianne (Shelley Long); and then there were the regulars like Norm (George Wendt), a guy with a big thirst who would do anything for a drink. An old man asked Norm what he would think if he bought someone in the bar a beer; Norm told him if he bought him a pitcher, he would give the guy a kiss on the lips!

In 1984, Rock Hudson kissed Linda Evans on the TV show *Dynasty*. Hudson had recently been diagnosed with AIDS. There was little knowledge and understanding of the disease, and fear that it could be transmitted via saliva. The kiss caused turmoil in Hollywood, and a frenzied panic that Evans could be endangered. The actress later revealed on *Larry King Live* that there were people on the set who wouldn't come near her, because they had children and didn't want to put them at risk.

The result was a 1985 Screen Actors Guild policy statement, requiring producers and agents to notify actors in advance if their roles required an open-mouthed kiss, as it could be "a possible hazard to the health of actors."

In 1986, television took on a new role, when the United States Senate voted to make cameras part of its proceedings. President Ronald Reagan, who had a lot of experience from his acting days, offered colleagues the following advice: "Learn your lines, don't bump into the furniture—and, in the kissing scenes, keep your mouth closed."

It was a great decade in movie kisstory. In *Star Wars: The Empire Strikes Back* (1980), Han Solo (Harrison Ford) asked Princess Leia (Carrie Fisher) if she was afraid he was going to leave her without saying goodbye. When she replied that she'd rather kiss a Wookie, he told her he would arrange it!

One of the best kissing quotes of all time was in the 1981 movie, *On Golden Pond*. Retired professor Norman Thayer (Henry Fonda) and his wife, Ethel (Katharine Hepburn) spent the summer at their cottage. When Norman had a mild heart attack, he got up and took his wife in his arms. Parroting his teenage grandson, he asked her if she wanted to dance, or if she would rather just "suck face"?

In 1982, Gertie (Drew Barrymore) gave E.T. in *E.T.: The Extra-Terrestrial* a very sweet kiss on the nose goodbye.

And in *Tootsie,* Michael (Dustin Hoffman) disguised himself as a woman in order to get an acting part; while in drag he attempted to kiss Julie (Jessica Lange), catching her totally off guard.

More than two decades before *Brokeback Mountain*, the movie *Deathtrap* (1982) featured a passionate kiss between Michael Caine and Christopher Reeve (the actors reportedly consumed copious amounts of alcohol to gear up for it). Producers later dubbed it the "ten million dollar kiss." That's the amount of money the movie lost due to negative publicity surrounding the lip-lock.

Another great kissing scene occurred in *Rain Man* (1988), which starred Dustin Hoffman as Raymond Babbitt, an autistic savant. Raymond had never been kissed, so one night, in an elevator at a Las Vegas casino, a friend, Susanna (Valeria Golino), taught him how. Afterward, she asked how it was. "Wet," was Raymond's reply.

There was also a "serial kisser" at large. In 1980, "serial kisser" Jose Alves de Moura, of Brazil, struck for the first time. He jumped on stage with Frank Sinatra and gave "Old Blue Eyes" a kiss. His list of victims since then includes Tony Bennett, Shirley MacLaine, soccer great Pelé, Jacques Cousteau, Pope John Paul II, and George Bush.

The hot-lipped Moura's goal is to achieve world peace, by kissing all the rich and famous people that he can (over 400 to date). But not everyone appreciates his unique way of extending an olive branch. Moura has been beaten on numerous occasions, and arrested over seventy-five times.

The 1990s

IF FACES HAD BEEN MEANT TO KISS EACH OTHER,
THEY WOULD NOT HAVE BEEN GIVEN NOSES.

—Bill Cosby (*Love and Marriage*, 1990)

he 1990s saw the emergence of Oprah's Book Club and *Chicken Soup for the Soul*. Tickle Me Elmo made an appearance, as did Beanie Babies and khaki pants. Tiger Woods won the Masters, and *Martha Stewart Living* appeared on newsstands.

Great kissing songs included "Kisses in the Wind" by Paula Abdul (1992); "The Perfect Kiss" by Bette Midler (1995); "Kiss from a Rose" by Seal (1994); "Hold Me, Thrill Me,

A kiss without a moustache is like beef without mustard. – *Italian proverb*

Kiss Me, Kill Me" by U2 (1995); and "Last Kiss" by Pearl Jam (1998).

On TV, a milestone was reached when the first female-female kiss occurred. In 1991, Cara Jean Lamb (Amanda Donohoe) kissed a female colleague on the lips on *L.A. Law*. Religious and right-wing groups were up in arms, and several sponsors pulled out. Perhaps it was the fact that TV comes right into our living rooms that made it seem so offensive; after all, the first such kiss in the movies had occurred in 1922!

Then, in 1994, Mariel Hemingway kissed Roseanne Barr on the popular TV show *Roseanne*. The episode was called "Don't Ask, Don't Tell," after the recently introduced law directed at military personnel keeping their sexuality hidden, if they wished to remain in their careers.

This time, much of the controversy surrounding the TV episode occurred *before* the kiss even aired. Network executives, fearful of losing advertising revenue, didn't want to air the controversial scene. Barr stood her ground. A gay-rights activist, and the executive producer of what was one of the most popular shows at the time, she threatened to move the series to another network. After much bickering, the kiss aired, with a viewer warning at the beginning of the episode. The publicity resulted in a rating bonanza: over 30 million viewers tuned in.

There were other TV kisses, as well. On *Friends*, Rachael (Jennifer Aniston) and Ross (David Schwimmer) had their first lip-lock at the local coffee shop. And on *Seinfeld*, Jerry complained to Kramer that just because he started to "kiss hello" the women in his apartment building, they expected him to do it all the time. The flabbergasted Jerry shouted at Kramer that he wouldn't be kissing those ladies anymore, and he didn't care what the consequences were. Kramer responded by grabbing Jerry's head in his hands and planting a big smooch on his lips!

There were some memorable movie kisses, as well.

In *Pretty Woman* (1990), there was the romantic (and totally improbable) tale of Vivian (Julia Roberts), a hooker with a heart of gold, who fell in love with Louis

(Richard Gere), the man who hired her as his companion for a week. The two fell in love, and instead of returning to New York, Louis climbed the fire escape and, with a passionate kiss, made all of Vivian's dreams come true.

In 1995, the Sleeping Beauty tale was reversed in the movie *Matrix*. This time it was Trinity (Carrie-Anne Moss) who came upon the lifeless body of Neo (Keanu Reeves). After Trinity professed to Neo her love for him, she gave him a loving kiss until he awakened—then screamed at him to get up!

In 1997, Jack Dawson (Leonardo DiCaprio) famously kissed Rose Dewitt (Kate Winslet) for the first time, on the prow of the ship in *Titanic*. They were bathed in the golden glow of the sunset—a view that transformed into a ghostly, underwater grave.

In 1999, Josie (Drew Barrymore) was an undercover reporter, who went back to her high school in *Never Been Kissed*. She fell in love with her high school teacher, who couldn't return her affection because he believed she was an underage student. Josie wrote him a letter,

Kissing Superstitions

◆ If you kiss someone on the nose, it will lead to a quarrel.

◆ To prevent a lightning strike, cross yourself three times and kiss the ground.

◆ If your nose is itchy, it means you will kiss a fool.

◆ If a single woman kisses a man with a moustache and gets some hair on her lips, she is doomed to be an old maid.

◆ The clinking of glasses before a kiss chases away evil spirits. Kiss someone at the stoke of midnight on New Year's Eve and you will have a year of luck in love.

◆ If you kiss someone on the cheek, you will be stabbed in the back.

◆ You can ward off a cold by kissing a mouse on the nose.

revealing the truth, and stated that she would stand on the pitcher's mound at the state championship baseball game for five minutes, prior to the first pitch, waiting for him. He rushed in at the last moment, and gave Josie her first real kiss.

The breath-freshening Smint candies, which sponsored the movie, conducted a survey prior to its release. They found that women compared kissing to "melted butter" or "being hit by a wave." Men, on the other hand, described it as similar to "vibrations at a concert," or a "three pointer at the buzzer to win the NCAA basketball tournament." Vive la difference!

But even in the nineties, kissing was not scandal-free. In 1990, the Beijing *Worker's Daily* advised that "the invasive Europeans brought the kissing custom to China, but it is regarded as a vulgar practice which is all too suggestive of cannibalism."

On the other side of the globe, in 1996, a teacher in Lexington, North Carolina, saw a first grader named Johnathan kiss a classmate on the cheek. The appalled teacher reported the incident to the school principal, who expelled the six year old for a day. This meant missing an ice cream party at school! For the record: Johnathan kissed the girl not only because he liked her, but because she had asked him to.

Still, it wasn't all doom and gloom in kisstory. In 1990, Alfred Wolfram kissed 8,001 people in eight hours, at the Minnesota Renaissance Festival. That's sixteen people every minute. (No mention on how much ChapStick was required for the feat!)

And, in 1997, some romantically-inclined researchers at Princeton University found that our brains are equipped with neurons to help us find our lover's lips in the dark!

We've Come a Long Way

HARRY LOOKED AROUND; THERE WAS GINNY RUNNING TOWARDS HIM; SHE HAD A HARD, BLAZING LOOK IN HER FACE AS SHE THREW HER ARMS AROUND HIM. AND WITHOUT THINKING, WITHOUT PLANNING IT, WITHOUT WORRYING ABOUT THE FACT THAT FIFTY PEOPLE WERE WATCHING, HARRY KISSED HER.

—J.K. Rowling (*Harry Potter and the Half-Blood Prince*, 2006)

 t seems like everywhere you look today, there is a whole lot of kissing going on.

Britney Spears kissed Madonna on the 2003 MTV Music Video Awards. Air kissing—or pretending to kiss, without actually touching

Love is a sudden revelation; a kiss is always a discovery. –anonymous

someone—is so common, that "mwah" is now officially a part of the dictionary.

Today, 90 percent of the world's population kisses. Even countries that once considered it a vulgar practice are now puckering up. In China, kissing contests are popular among teenagers, challenging the traditional view that it should be a private affair. In Indonesia, the film *Arisa* (2003) showed the first homosexual screen kiss. Although not everyone was comfortable with the subject matter, critics loved the movie, and the religious right remained surprisingly silent. And if you happen to be in Korea on June 14, happy "Kiss Day" to you.

There are Guinness World Records, including the longest kiss (thirty-one hours, thirty minutes, and thirty seconds) and for the most couples kissing at once: 7,451. SkyEurope Airlines proved love was flying high on Valentine's Day, 2008: they encouraged passengers on eighty-four flights to kiss in mid air. A total of 2,214 kisses were counted; participants were awarded a voucher toward a free ticket, and all passengers received little chocolate hearts.

Today, 70 percent of people experience their first kiss by the age of fifteen (only 46 percent of their parents can say the same). Online, there are a myriad of websites: a Google search of "kiss" yields over 243 million results! There are e-kisses, virtual kissing booths, "how to" advice, and blogs. There's a World Kissing Day—although when it occurs is a tricky question. April 28, June 6, and November 11 have all been cited. I guess to be safe, one should smooch every day of the year!

On TV, a new barrier was broken in 2000. The first female-female kiss occurred on *L.A. Law* in 1991 (and shows like *Picket Fences*, *Ellen*, *Friends*, *Ally McBeal*, and *Party of Five* have followed suit since then), but it took almost another decade for the first kiss between two males to come about.

On the hit show *Will and Grace*, Jack (Sean Hayes) eagerly told Will (Eric McCormack) that there was going to be a kiss between two gay men for the first time on prime-time TV. They turned on the television, settled in for the big event, and waited. But just as the kiss was about to happen—the camera panned away from the actors and focused on the fireplace instead! Outraged, Jack talked Will into appearing on *The Today Show* to protest censorship. Jack whined about how long it was going to take to see a gay kiss on TV. After Will told Jack it wouldn't be as long as he thought, he impetuously grabbed Jack, and gave him a passionate kiss!

In movies, there was the great kiss in the 2002 blockbuster *Spiderman*. While standing in the pouring rain, Mary-Jane (Kirsten Dunst) watched as the costumed hero (Tobey Maguire) hung upside down on the fire escape. Mary-Jane thanked Spiderman for saving her life by slowly peeling back the lower part of his mask and planting a heartfelt kiss on his eager lips.

In *Brokeback Mountain* (2005), Ennis del Mar (Heath Ledger) and Jack Twist (Jake Gyllenhaal) were herding cattle on an isolated mountain in Wyoming. The first kiss between them was a tender, tentative one, as both men explored their sexuality and blossoming feelings for each other. Four years later, when they met again, they shared a much more urgent one.

In teen literature, romance is in full bloom, thanks to the books (and movies based on them) by Stephanie Meyer. In *Twilight*, Edward asked, "Are you still faint from the rain? Or was it my kissing expertise?" And in the novel *Breaking Dawn*, Bella said, "I couldn't speak anymore. I lifted my head and kissed him with a passion that might possibly set the forest on fire."

Researchers continue to give us more reasons to pucker up. A passionate kiss uses thirty-four facial muscles, toning the neck and jaw. It burns twenty-six calories a minute, reduces stress, and can increase your heart rate—which is similar to a good cardiovascular workout, but a lot more fun! And swapping saliva (which contains fat, mineral salts, and protein) can bolster the production of antibodies, to help ward off disease.

Kissing improves the circulation in your skin, and reduces rashes and blemishes, leaving you with a glowing complexion (as well as a twinkle in your eye!).

Not Out of the Woods Yet

OH WHAT LIES LURK IN KISSING.

—Heinrich Heine

n 2004, the British TV show *Big Brother* was filmed in the kingdom of Bahrain, a tiny island-state in the Persian Gulf. At the beginning of the first episode, the handsome Abdel Hakim greeted a young woman named Kawthar with a kiss on the cheek. It proved to be a "kiss of death" for the show. In Islamic countries, laws do not permit unmarried couples to have any sort of physical relationship, and touching and kissing are definitely taboo. The outrage over the "transgression" was so great that the show was axed two weeks after it had debuted. This isn't the only incident of infamous modern-day kissing.

In 2005, an Israeli couple met in India and married in a traditional Hindu ceremony there. When they hugged and kissed during the chanting of a religious verse, priests filed a case, saying they had offended Hindu sentiments. The couple was apologetic, stating they were unaware that public kissing was banned. They paid the 1,000 rupees fine (about twenty-two dollars) rather than the alternative —spending ten days in jail!

In 2007, Richard Gere kissed the popular Bollywood actress Shilpa Shetty on the cheek at a televised event promoting AIDS awareness in India. Islamic fundamentalists were enraged. They demanded an apology from Shetty, and threatened to ban her movies. People burned effigies of Gere, and a judge charged him with committing an "obscene act" in a public place and issued a warrant for his arrest (the arrest order was finally stayed in 2008).

In Indonesia, would-be kissers beware! A law prohibits public displays of affection and is punishable with up to five years in jail. In Malaysia, Kuala Lumpur mayor Roslin Hassan assured tourists that they would be exempt from indecency charges, after a federal court decided to prosecute a Chinese couple for holding hands and kissing in a park. "We will not harass tourists for kissing in public, but it better not be the passionate kind," the mayor said.

Even dignitaries are not above the kissing fray. In 2007, when Iranian President Mahmoud Ahmadinejad kissed the gloved hand of an elderly teacher during a celebration of Iranian Teacher's Day, he was sharply rebuked. Islamic newspapers noted that under Shariah law, contact with a woman who is unrelated is a crime that can be punishable by death.

It's not only in Islamic countries that controversial kisses occur. Russian President Vladimir Putin was on a walkabout, when he crouched down beside a small boy to chat. Then, suddenly, he lifted the child's shirt, kissed him on the stomach, then patted the boy on the head and walked off. Onlookers were shocked, radio talk shows were abuzz, and the kiss constantly replayed on TV. "It was like touching a kitten," Putin later tried to explain.

This wasn't the President's only bizarre kiss. While visiting a fish farm, a photo was taken of Putin planting a peck on the head of a sturgeon. Perhaps it was his way of saying "thanks" to the type of fish that produces the best caviar.

In France, a woman went on trial after she kissed an all-white painting by American artist Cy Twombly, valued at two million dollars, smearing it with her red lipstick. She was tried in court for "voluntary degradation of a work of art," and ordered to pay a fine to the painter's owner and the gallery. The woman said "it was an act of love"; prosecutors called it "a sort of cannibalism."

In Italy, gay activists staged a "kiss-in" after two men were arrested for kissing in front of the Colosseum. And the American Broadcasting Company cut the kisses between the two male characters from *Brokeback Mountain* when it aired on TV. Representatives of the station said the scenes were "accidentally left out"—but no such "mistakes" were made with the heterosexual scenes, which aired in their original form.

In the United States, there was an infamous presidential kiss. Following George Bush's State of the Union Address in 2005, the Republican president grabbed Democratic Senator Joe Lieberman's head in his hand, and leaned in close to his cheek. "The kiss," as it became known, became a political hot potato; Lieberman denied a kiss had occurred; critics said it was evidence of his too-close relationship with Bush.

In 2007, a high school picture of two teenage boys kissing was blacked out of a New Jersey yearbook, after it was deemed inappropriate. And for a country that considers itself forward thinking, there are some pretty quaint kissing laws still on the books in America. For example:

◆ In Iowa, a man with a moustache may never kiss a woman in public.

◆ In Logan County, Colorado, it is

illegal for a man to kiss a woman while she is asleep.

◆ A man in Florida may not kiss his wife's breast.

◆ Two people may not kiss in front of any church in Massachusetts.

◆ In Wisconsin, it is illegal to kiss on a train.

◆ Kisses on the lips are against the local health ordinance in Riverside, California—unless both parties wipe their lips with carbonized rose water.

Despite the health benefits of kissing, there are some drawbacks to a good lip-lock. And though they don't warrant a Doctor's Warning—yet!—those in the Lonely Hearts Club may take solace in this: A kiss can contain up to 278 different types of bacteria. Most are not dangerous, but sometimes "swapping spit" can lead to tuberculosis, colds, scarlet fever, bronchitis, boils and abscesses, herpes, hepatitis B, and mononucleosis (also known as the "kissing disease"). A passionate kiss can raise hormone levels in the blood so much that it can shorten life by a full minute.

In 2007, Egyptian pediatrician Dr. Adel Ashur started the No

Kisses After Today group, explaining that a kiss on the cheek could lead to the spread of the avian flu. The good doctor also says parents should not kiss their children before they are fourteen years old. The reason: a child's immune system is not completely developed until then, so a well-meaning smooch could lead to infections and disease.

Perhaps Dr. Ashur should enlist the help of the Kissing Shield. This is a germ barrier made of latex and stretched over a heart-shaped frame. The inventor claims it is useful for those who enjoy kissing, but dread getting diseases. The Kissing Shield is patented—but not yet produced. No word when (or if) it will be coming to a store near you.

The Future of Kisstory

KISSING IS THE WAY TO PARADISE.

—Greek proverb

t is true that nobody knows what the future will bring. But if the past is any indication, kissing is in for a long—and perhaps bumpy—ride.

There will be more record kisses (space kissing contests, anyone?), more barriers broken, more books to be written, and songs to be sung. And people the world over will continue to be delighted, amazed—and appalled—at this ever-simple yet meaningful endearment.

Perhaps Homer and Marge

A bite from a loving mouth is worth more than a kiss from any other. —Lebanese proverb

Simpson hold the greatest wisdom of all. In *The Simpsons Movie* (2007), they shared a kiss as they drove on a motorcycle. Afterward, Marge purred that it was the best kiss of her life. "So far," Homer replied. Then they rode off into the sunset together.

The End . . . but not quite!

For there is one part of kisstory that is yet to be written, and it is perhaps the greatest story of all— your own!

Credits:

p. 6: ©Christie's Images/SuperStock

p. 12: ©Pushkin Museum, Moscow, Russia/The Bridgeman Art Library

p. 18: ©The Art Archive/Archaeological Museum Tarquinia/Gianni Dagli Orti

p. 27: ©Castello della Manta, Saluzzo, Italy/Alinari/The Bridgeman Art Library

p. 34: Art Gallery and Museum, Kelvingrove, Glasgow, Scotland/© Culture and Sport Glasgow (Museums)/The Bridgeman Art Library

p. 45: Private Collection/©Look and Learn/The Bridgeman Art Library

p. 51: ©Simon Carter Gallery, Woodbridge, Suffolk, UK/The Bridgeman Art Library

p. 56: ©Linda Braucht/Superstock

p. 62: Private Collection/©The Stapleton Collection/The Bridgeman Art Library

p. 71: ©Mary Evans Picture Library

p. 78: Private Collection/©The Advertising Archives/The Bridgeman Art Library

p. 86: ©Jason Laure/The Image Works

p. 95: Courtesy Everett Collection

p. 98: Courtesy Everett Collection

p. 107: ©20th Century Fox/Paramount/ The Kobal Collection

p. 112: ©Scott Gries/Getty Images

p. 121: ©Matt Dunn/SuperStock

p. 126: Painting by Dora Holzhandler. ©Private Collection/The Bridgeman Art Library

Illuminated manuscript type, ©iStockphoto.com/jusant: pp. 7, 13, 19, 25, 35, 43, 49, 57, 63, 69, 79, 87, 93, 99, 105, 113, 119, 127

Frame, ©iStockphoto.com/leezsnow: pp. 18, 51, 78, 107

Frame, ©iStockphoto.com/Rouzes: pp. 6, 34, 62, 95, 121

Frame, ©iStockphoto.com/winterling: pp. 12, 44, 71, 98, 126

Frame, ©iStockphoto.com/dareknie: pp. 27, 56, 86, 112